Did you know that there are more than 5,000 kinds of frogs? Each one is different, but they have some things in common.

All frogs have short bodies, big back legs, smaller front legs, and no tail. Almost all of them can jump, but some can only manage short hops. They eat small animals like snails, slugs, worms, beetles, and flies.

Frogs do some of their breathing through their skin, and they usually live in damp places. Most kinds are found in warm parts of the world where it rains a lot. The ones that live where the winter is cold, like much of North America and Europe, hibernate and come out in spring to breed.

Almost all frogs lay eggs—usually in ponds or streams—that hatch into tadpoles with tails and no legs. They don't look anything like their parents.

As a tadpole grows older, its tail begins to shrink and it starts to sprout back and front legs.

Eventually the tail disappears and the tadpole becomes a tiny frog.

Fabulous
Martin Jenkins

For
Richard & Adrian
T. H.

For
my family
M. J.

CANDLEWICK PRESS

Text copyright © 2015 by Martin Jenkins. Illustrations copyright © 2015 by Tim Hopgood. All rights reserved. No part of this book may be reproduced, transmitted, or stored in an information retrieval system in any form or by any means, graphic, electronic, or mechanical, including photocopying, taping, and recording, without prior written permission from the publisher. First U.S. edition 2016. Library of Congress Catalog Card Number 2015932371. ISBN 978-0-7636-8100-5. This book was typeset in Avenir and Imperfect. The illustrations were done in mixed media. Candlewick Press, 99 Dover Street, Somerville, Massachusetts 02144.   visit us at www.candlewick.com. Printed in Johor Bahru, Malaysia. 15 16 17 18 19 20 TWP 10 9 8 7 6 5 4 3 2 1

MIX
Paper from
responsible sources
FSC
www.fsc.org
FSC® C012700

Frogs

illustrated by

Tim Hopgood

This frog is **huge**

(for a frog).

It's a goliath frog, and it lives in western Africa. It's the biggest frog in the world. Sometimes it eats other frogs!

These frogs are tiny.

This is the smallest kind of frog in the world, or at least the smallest that anybody knows about.
It lives in Papua New Guinea.

And this one has a very strange nose.

It's called Darwin's frog, and it lives in South America. No one really knows why it has a pointy nose.

oops . . .

This frog can . . .

jump really far,
really quickly.

It's a striped rocket frog from Australia.
It can jump sixteen feet (five meters) in
one go—very handy for escaping from
enemies in a hurry.

croak

ribbit

honk

And these ones make an awful lot of noise.

rack-rack

churp

Frogs call to let other frogs know they are there.
These are all male frogs. Female frogs are generally
much quieter. The big one in the middle is a bullfrog.

This one is called
a flying frog,
although it can't
really fly.

It lives in trees in forests in Southeast Asia.
It spreads out the skin between its toes to help it
float in the air when it jumps from tree to tree.

16

And this one is called a hairy frog, although it doesn't have any real hair.

The hairy frog lives in western Africa. The things that look like hairs are little strips of skin. They probably help the frog breathe when it's underwater.

I think these frogs
are all very beautiful.

I couldn't tell you which one
is the *most*
beautiful.

But I can tell you that each one could kill a horse, though only if the horse was silly enough to try to eat it.

A horse wouldn't eat a frog on purpose, but plenty of other animals might. South American poison arrow frogs have deadly poison in their skin to help protect them. Their bright colors are a way of saying "Keep away!"

19

These frogs make
a nest of foam for their eggs.

They're African gray tree frogs. Their nests hang in branches over ponds or streams.
When the eggs in the nests hatch, the tadpoles wriggle out and drop into the water below.

And the one with the very strange nose looks after its babies in its throat!

The male Darwin's frog snaps up the eggs just before they hatch and keeps the tadpoles in a special pouch in his throat. You'd think he would swallow them all the way down by accident, but he never seems to.

This frog never leaves the water.

It's an African clawed frog.
It spends its whole life living in a stream
or pond. Not many frogs do that.

And this frog can live buried in the ground for years and years . . .

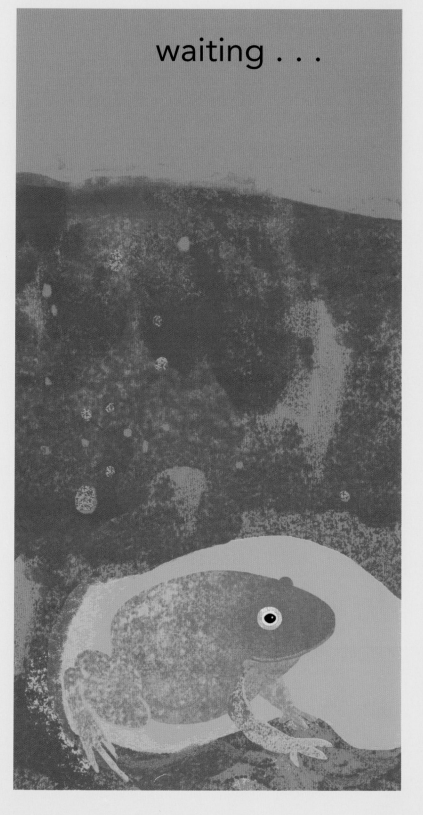

waiting . . .

for the rain.

It's an Australian water-holding frog, and it lives in the desert. It makes a little room for itself where it stays cool and damp. When it rains and the ground gets wet, the frog digs itself out.

All

these frogs are wonderful, but . . .

25

my favorite frog of all is the medium-size,
greeny-brown one that sits on a lily pad
in my backyard pond!

Martin Jenkins and **Tim Hopgood** wanted to get as many frogs as possible into this book, so here are a few more, just for fun:

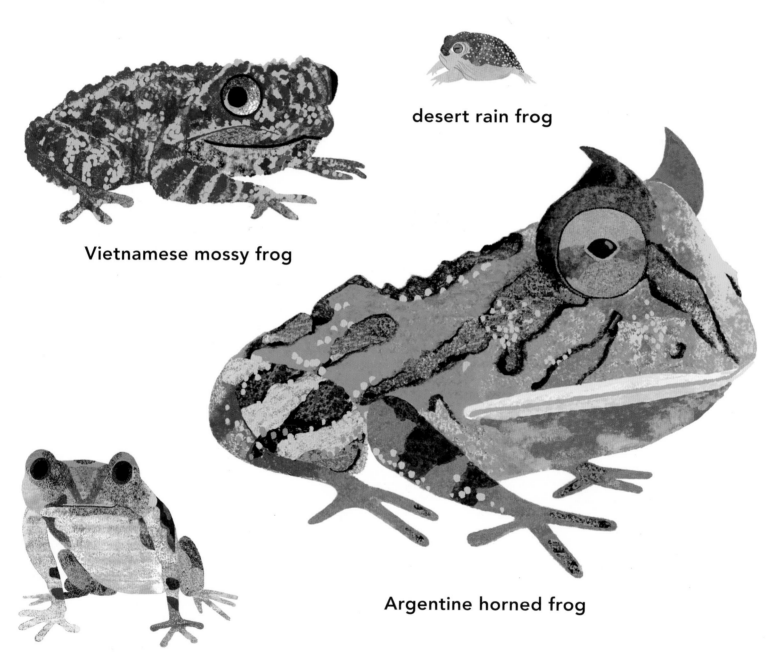

desert rain frog

Vietnamese mossy frog

Argentine horned frog

Malagasy rainbow frog

painted reed frog

whitebelly reed frog

splendid leaf frog

black rain frog

Index

Look up the pages to find out about all these froggy things. Don't forget to look at both kinds of words— **this kind** and this kind.

breathing 17

digging 23

eating 9

eggs 20, 21

jumping 14, 16

noise 15

nose 12

poison 19

pond 20, 22, 27

tadpoles 20, 21

throat 21

MORE INFORMATION

Martin Jenkins says the best place to find out about frogs is **amphibiaweb.org.** You can also find a lot of useful information at **iucnredlist.org** and **arkive.org,** and on Wikipedia.

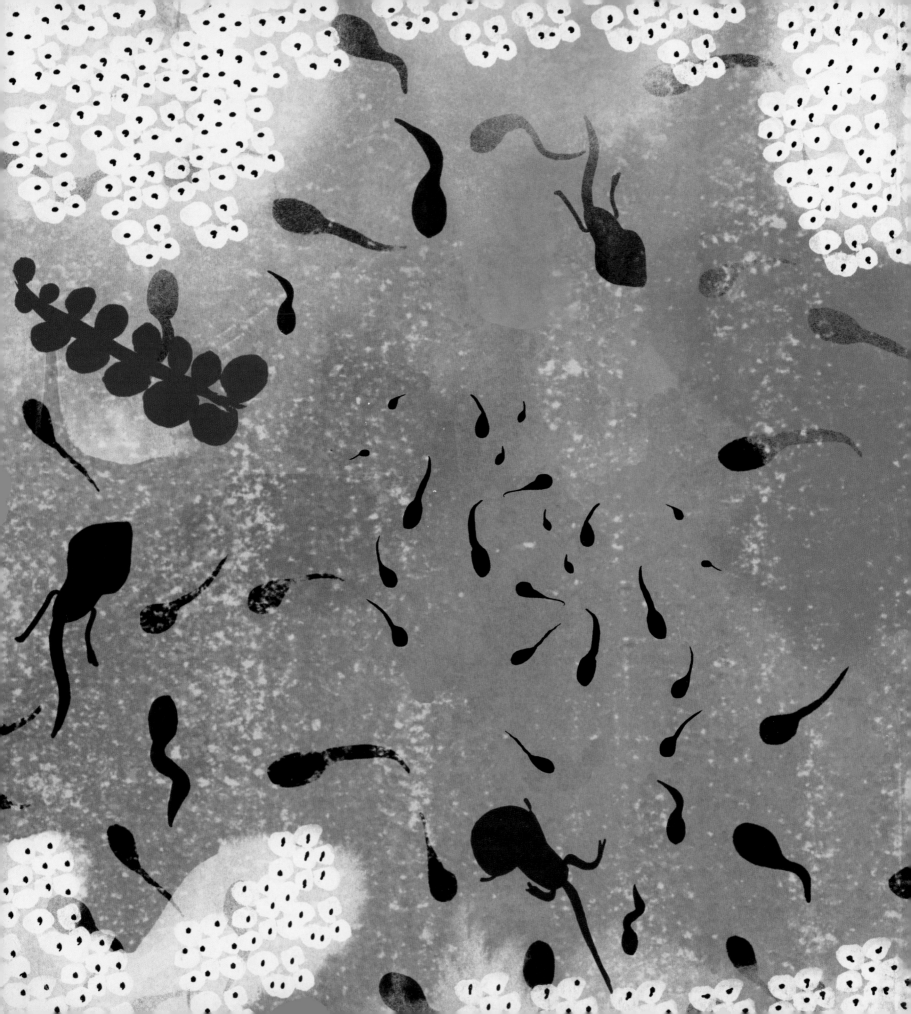